Looking at Aztec Myths and Legends

Land
of the
Five Suns

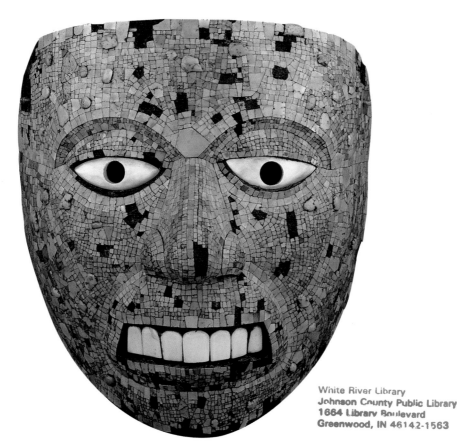

Kay McManus

NTC *Publishing Group*
Lincolnwood, Illinois USA

How to say Aztec names

The long Aztec names look difficult at first but they are not too hard to say if you read them slowly and pronounce each letter. This list will help you:

Ahuitzotl	A-hweet-zot-ell
Chalchiuhtlicue	Chal-chee-oot-li-kay
Coatepec	Co-a-tep-eck
Coatlicue	Co-at-li-kay
Coyolxauhqui	Co-yoll-sho-kay
Huitzilopochtli	Hweet-sill-o-posht-lee
Mictlantecuhtli	Micked-lan-te-koot-lee
Nanahuatzin	Na-na-oo-at-sin
Quetzalcoatl	Kwet-zall-co-at-ell
Tamoanchan	Tam-o-an-chan
Tecuciztecatl	Te-koo-sis-te-cat-ell
Tezcatlipoca	Tex-cat-lee-poke-a
Tlaloc	Te-la-lock
Tonacatepetl	Ton-a-cat-e-petal
Xiuhcoatl	Shee-oo-ko-at-ell
Xochipilli	Sosh-ee-pill-ee
Xochiquetzal	Sho-shee-ket-sal
Yacatecuhtli	Ya-ka-te-koot-lee

Published by NTC Publishing Group
4255 West Touhy Avenue, Lincolnwood (Chicago), Illinois 60646-1975, U.S.A.

First published in the United Kingdom in 1996 by British Museum Press

Designed by Carla Turchini
Printed in Slovenia

Front cover: Aztec turquoise mosaic serpent pectoral.

Contents

About the Aztecs

The Aztec people were the most powerful nation in Mexico 500 years ago. They built a great capital city called Tenochtitlan and many other peoples had to pay tribute to them. Aztec traders, called pochteca, traveled far and wide and were men of influence and power.

The Aztec empire lasted until 1521, when Hernando Cortés and his Spanish soldiers came to Tenochtitlan. At first the Aztecs welcomed the Spanish, but later they fought them fiercely and the Aztecs were defeated.

Our story begins in the year 1521, before the Spanish invaders arrived in Tenochtitlan.

The long search

Of all my brothers, it is the small restless one we call Two Rabbit Leaping Frog who causes the most pain and worry to his mother and to all our family living here in our island city of Tenochtitlan.

I, Stone Turtle, am the middle son of my father and am proud to be part of such an important family whose name is honoured among all the other pochteca. The name of pochteca itself means "the merchants who lead," and my father has led many traders on their journeys to the distant cities of our kingdom. Now he no longer makes such journeys himself, but commands the other traders who come over the causeways to sell their goods in our city markets.

Soon, when I have finished school, I shall be making such journeys myself. I shall carry back to Tenochtitlan not only cotton and cacao but precious feathers and turquoise. Perhaps then, like my father, I shall be known to all the noble lords of this city, and perhaps even to the commanders of the fierce jaguar and eagle warriors, too. So you will understand now why our family is so important and why my father is a man of power and knowledge whose words must always be obeyed.

Generally his words are obeyed but not always by Leaping Frog. I suppose that when I was casting a shadow of the same size I, too, angered my mother and father by playing in the dust when I should have been helping to carry water or gather reeds. Still, I'm sure that I never disappeared as quickly as my brother Leaping Frog does whenever there is work to be done!

If I am at home and not at school when he is lost, I am always the one who is sent to look for him. Leaping Frog is not a brother who is easy to find, for he seems to have friends everywhere. Perhaps it will be better when he, too, starts school because then he will have other people to watch him and to make him listen to the things they say.

Our mother says that Leaping Frog only listens to me because he likes to hear my stories. It was my mother who chose to use the name of Leaping Frog. He has his other names, of course, but she said he was just like a leaping frog – one minute he is there crouching by your foot and then, within a breath, he is lost and hidden in the reeds. So the name has stayed with him.

He was lost again today which is when I thought about looking for him among the reeds or near water. That is why I went first to the nearest of the chinampas, the raised fields that stand like islands above the water. Leaping Frog has always liked watching the farmers, digging and planting their crops, so I listened all the time for the sound of his voice as I made my

This splendid ornament is made of wood covered with turquoise mosaic. It is probably part of a ceremonial costume – either a headdress or an ornament worn on the chest. It is quite large – about 17 inches across.

Turquoise was one of the precious raw materials traded over hundreds of miles. Traders traveled far to the north, way beyond the boundaries of the Aztec Empire, into what is now the south west of the United States. The journeys involved great hardship and danger for the pochteca who carried the turquoise back to the city of Tenochtitlan.

Because of its importance, turquoise was reserved for the ruler and the most important families to use in their religious ceremonies and festivals.

way past the lines of willows that edge the banks of the canal.

On my way I spoke to two of the workers who were driving new stakes of wood into the mud. They laughed when I told them who I was looking for.

"You should tell your brother that he must never become a warrior. He would lose his way on any battlefield and his enemy would have to search for him!"

Their words angered me so I turned away and was about to give up my search when I heard a cry. It came from beyond some trees edging a chinampa, green with new maize.

I called out as I ran. "Leaping Frog – where are you?"

Bending down, I pulled back the reeds and saw that he had slipped down between the wooden strips that formed a bridge over the canal. He grabbed my hand and I saw that one of his feet, which was already bleeding, was held fast by the splintered wood. In fact he really did look like a small frog, dangling and dripping above the darkening water.

He was sobbing now. "I saw the water beast!" he said. "I saw Ahuitzotl. He's over there – look! In the blackness under the trees. He was going to grab me and drown me!"

I glanced across towards the trees. Did I see something move in the shadows? I had heard enough stories about the water beast to know that I did not want my brother to be his next victim. The water under the trees seemed to shudder suddenly and Leaping Frog gave another cry of terror.

In panic, I reached down and put my hand deep into the water, carefully easing away the sharp point of the broken wood. A further swirl of blood followed my hand, and I suddenly felt the weight of Leaping Frog's body as I began to pull him up on to the bank.

"I saw him, Stone Turtle. He was there! All the time he was there!" And then he said suddenly, "I hate water. Why do we live in such a city of water?"

"You should be proud to live here," I said. "Don't you remember the story I told you about how this wonderful city was first built?"

He stopped crying at once. "I can remember some of it," he said, "but if you tell me again, I will remember it all, won't I?"

I knew that he had not forgotten one word but as I carried him home, I told him once more the story of Tenochtitlan and

of our ancestors who had traveled from the lands of the north
to find the site for their new home. He fell asleep before we
had gone very far, but I finished the story, not only because I
wanted to forget that he was heavy in my arms, but because it
is important that such accounts are held on people's lips or
carved in stone so that they are never forgotten.

The founding of Tenochtitlan

Long, long ago our ancestors lived on an island in a distant
part of our land on a lake which was called Aztlan, the
place of the birds. They lived among mountains and lakes and
listened always to the words of their god of war, the great
Huitzilopochtli. They fished and hunted and grew their crops,
and carried out the wishes of their gods that were spoken
through the mouths of their priests. And so it seemed to our
ancestors that they would live in Aztlan forever and that their
sons would live in those same mountains until the end of their
days.

Then one day, the priests called them all to listen to some
new words that Huitzilopochtli had spoken and they realized
that nothing would ever be the same again.

"Huitzilopochtli says you must leave this place," said the
priests. "You must leave behind all your mountains and your
caves, your rivers and your springs of clear water, and you
must leave them for ever."

Now the people who were our fathers had been happy in
their island home in Lake Aztlan. But they all knew that they
must listen to the words of their god.

"You will leave this place," said Huitzilopochtli, "and you
will take with you all your bows and your arrows and your
fishing nets, and you will become nomads traveling through
the land until you come to the place that will become the new
home of your people."

And so it was that our ancestors carried out the wishes of the
great god, Huitzilopochtli. They left the mountains and the
caves, and all the rivers and the streams that they had known
before, and started on their long journey. They crossed through

unknown lands and over strange and untrodden hills and often they were tired and longed for the journey to be over.

Sometimes they found places that had fertile land and they stopped and built temples and began to grow crops again, but always the priests kept reminding them of what Huitzilopochtli had said.

"This is not the place," they said. "He will give us a sign when we have reached the site where our people are to settle. He will show us clearly, and there we shall build a temple to Huitzilopochtli and there shall we make our home."

"But how shall we know?" said the people. "What sort of sign will our great leader give us?"

"We shall recognize the sign," said the priests, "and we shall establish ourselves and will become the lords and kings of all that is in the world."

As time passed, the journey became no easier and many of the people grew discontented with their life as nomads. Often they had to defend themselves against wild animals and attacks by local tribes. They even quarreled among themselves. One group began to demand a more settled way of life, and finally, they were abandoned by the rest who left them to seek their own way.

On and on, the men from Aztlan traveled. Children were born and grew older, and old men became impatient, looking for the sign that was to confirm the end of the journey. Eventually they came to this great valley in which we now live, but their troubles were far from over.

Many great battles had to be fought against their neighbors. One of the battles was against the forces of Copil, who was the new leader of the group of Aztecs that had gone off to settle by themselves. Our ancestors were victorious and Copil was captured and sacrificed, his heart taken out and hurled over the waters of a great lake on to a rocky island.

As time passed, the pilgrims almost gave up hope of ever reaching their promised home, until one day the priests announced that they had seen new visions and could hear again the voice of Huitzilopochtli.

"I shall appear as a white eagle," the god said, "and when

This picture from an Aztec book shows the founding of the city of Tenochtitlan. In the middle an eagle is sitting on a cactus, just as the god said.

Canals divide the city into four quarters.

At the bottom, the fighting warriors and burning pyramids show the Aztecs conquering two other cities.

The first king of Tenochtitlan is sitting to the left of the cactus and you can also see his nine noble advisers. The boxes in the border stand for the years that the first king of Tenochtitlan reigned (1325-1375). The Aztec calendar was very complicated and each year had a number and a name. Count the small circles to find the year number. Can you find the box for year Two Rabbit?

you come to a place where it shall seem good to me that you stay, there I shall alight." And he told the priests that they must travel to the sacred island where Copil's heart had been thrown. There they would see an eagle land on a cactus growing from a rock and this would be the place that he had chosen to be their home.

And so the pilgrims, when they came at last to this sacred site and saw the eagle on a cactus just as the god had foretold, knew that their long journey was over.

Rejoicing, they laid down their bows and arrows. "Here we shall build our houses and our temples," they said. "This shall be our home!"

They called their new home Tenochtitlan, a place of rock and cactus, and there they built the city that was to become for all time the honored home of our people.

The fifth sun

I knew that Leaping Frog was lost again when I could no longer hear the sound of his drum.

My mother always says that it wakens her long before the first morning birds begin to call from our orchard. Often the drum goes on beating until the final moment when Leaping Frog stretches out on his mat again to sleep. Although it is quite a small drum, it seems to fill our heads with noise and irritation.

Sometimes when we are all tired of the noise, my mother sends him out to gather wood. Then, while he is away, she hides it. When he comes back and can't find the drum he looks so unhappy that she forgets her anger and pretends that she has just found it again. None of us likes to think about the day when Leaping Frog grows older and goes to a House of Song to learn how to play one of the large wooden drums. I am sure he will want to learn because I've watched his face when we've listened to the sound of those big drums that are played when the warriors dance to the Great Temple with their captives.

I was never given a drum to play, but then, exciting things always seem to happen to Leaping Frog! One day when he was playing with his friends near the flower market he met a trader who was looking for my father. He said he wanted to speak to him. I would have told such a man that my father was far too important to be called to speak to a stranger, but of course, Leaping Frog – whose tongue is never still – said he would go at once to find him. The man was so pleased that he took the small drum from the pack on his back and gave it to Leaping Frog. Afterwards, I thought it was strange that my father allowed my brother to keep the drum, but all he said was that the trader had brought him news from the coast that was far more important than the noise made by a child.

When I returned from school today, there was no sign of Leaping Frog or the drum. Apparently, the whole household was already looking for him but he was nowhere to be found.

The beating of drums was an important part of Aztec ritual and ceremony. Aztecs loved music, and drums provided the exciting rhythm for their dancing and chanting during festivals, and at times of family celebration.

Unlike Leaping Frog's small drum, this two-note wooden drum was a sacred instrument played at religious ceremonies.

Can you see the owl's face on the drum? Aztecs believed that the owl was a messenger from the underworld and the land of the gods. So perhaps this drum was used when people performed ceremonies in honor of the gods.

There had been rumors all day that our eagle and jaguar warriors had returned from a new battle and I knew the reports were true. Already our island causeways were crowded with people making their way towards the Great Temple. It was obvious that today many new captives would be following the path of sacrifice as our gods did when they first created human life.

I told my mother that I would look for my brother and I set off at once, my fear already hurrying my footsteps as I ran. As I came nearer to the Great Temple, I could see the warriors in their brilliantly colored cloaks. They were leading their captives, and I felt myself being swept forward by the press of bodies around me. I wanted to be part of all the clamor and excitement, letting myself be drowned in the noise and terror of the moment. It was difficult to make myself remember that I was looking for Leaping Frog.

I glanced around, not knowing which way to go, then noticed a small space beside the wall ahead. Jostling and pushing, I at last reached what looked like a heap of rags thrown over a small mound.

Angry in my relief, I pulled aside the rags. Leaping Frog's head was bleeding, and I saw that the small mound beside him was formed by the splintered pieces of his drum.

"Why did you come here alone?" I said. "Why do you always cause so much trouble?"

He sat up. "I wanted to see the captives," he said. "And I did, Stone Turtle. I saw them!"

I looked again at the advancing crowd. It was even larger now. How easily my brother could have been squashed against the wall, his own bones as splintered and crushed as his drum.

"I got really close," he said. "The captives were covered in dust and some could hardly walk. But they saw me playing my drum, and one of them smiled at me. After that I got pushed away and I could hear shouting and then there was darkness and I don't remember any more."

His face had grown paler, and I saw blood trickling through his hair, marking his neck with narrow threads of scarlet. I knew that it is always possible to die whenever a wound is deep enough. There was no time to be lost. Forcing my way through the flow of bodies, and with my brother in my arms, I managed somehow to find enough space to move away from the crowds and to reach the shadows of an old orchard not far from our own part of the city.

"My head hurts," said Leaping Frog. "You made it hurt as you ran."

I laid him down on the grass, and wiped away some of the blood with a few leaves.

"The pain will go," I said, "because I'm going to tell you a story."

I could see that his eyes were beginning to close. "Is it about a drum?" he said.

"No, it's about four different suns and about our own fifth one. And when the story is finished, we shall be home again and I shall mend your drum."

I had never thought that I would want to hear the beat of his drum again. But, as I began the story, I suddenly discovered that all that mattered was that Leaping Frog, too, should hear that sound again.

Land of the Five Suns

A long time ago before time began, there was only darkness. In this great ocean of space, all the gods gathered together and decided that a world must be created to fill this emptiness.

Now the two brother gods, whose names were Quetzalcoatl and Tezcatlipoca, could not agree about this first world, nor about the creatures who would live under its sun. As you and I know, Leaping Frog, brothers do not always agree, and Quetzalcoatl and Tezcatlipoca fought and quarreled and argued just as we do sometimes. But, of course, each of them was a powerful god and their battles caused great destruction and chaos.

In the beginning, it was Tezcatlipoca who got his own way and ruled over the first of all the worlds. He created a world, and its sun was called the sun of earth. Then he created giants to stride across its land. The giants were so tall and strong that they could tear up the trees of the forest with their bare hands. They never tilled the soil or learned to grow maize, but lived only on

This mask is made from a human skull covered in tiny pieces of stone and shell.

The black stripes tell us that it is meant to represent the god Tezcatlipoca, Smoking Mirror. He usually wears a black striped mask. His emblem was a black obsidian mirror. Some Aztec books show Tezcatlipoca with a mirror instead of one foot. This mirror allowed him to see everyone and everything happening in all places.

Obsidian is a form of brittle, volcanic glass. Aztec priests used obsidian mirrors to foretell the future.

wild fruits and the roots of plants. The name of this first world was Four Jaguar and the sun shone on its giants until one day Quetzalcoatl, who was still angry with his brother, took a great staff and struck down the god Tezcatlipoca so that he fell into the sea.

"Good! That is the end of Tezcatlipoca," thought Quetzalcoatl, the plumed serpent. "That is the end of my brother."

He was wrong! In the next instant, Tezcatlipoca rose out of the sea and became a jaguar. The jaguar was so strong and beautiful that it leapt into the sky where it can still be seen among the stars. Then the jaguars that were living in that first world also grew angry, so angry that they devoured every single one of the giants.

Out of this first destruction, Quetzalcoatl, the god of wind, created a new world which was called Four Wind. This time it

was Quetzalcoatl who ruled over its lands. But
Tezcatlipoca was still waiting and watching. And he
watched as this second sun shone over this second
world and his anger grew until one day he fought
another battle with his brother, our great god,
Quetzalcoatl. And Tezcatlipoca won this battle! Then
a great hurricane swept across the land, destroying
everything in its path, even the sun itself. It swept
away all the people of this second world, and to
this day, we can still see their descendants, the
monkeys who swing and climb among our tall
forest trees.

It was a different god, though, who ruled over
the third of our worlds. It was Tlaloc, the god of
rain, who is one of the most ancient of gods, and
he ruled over this third creation which is known as
the sun of rain. Its sun shone over its lands while
Tlaloc poured out the precious water that gave it life
and nourishment, and filled its lakes and rivers.
Again Quetzalcoatl became the destroyer, for he ended
this third world, too, by causing a rain of fire to fall over
the land. It burned and consumed everything on which it
fell, until its heat magically transformed all the beings
who lived there, turning them into turkeys before its own
third sun was finally destroyed.

Once more, out of destruction another world was created,
giving life to a fourth sun, the sun of water, and it was the wife
of Tlaloc who ruled over this new world. Her name was
Chalchiuhtlicue – She of the Jade Skirt – who as you will know,
Leaping Frog, is the goddess of streams and all standing water,
as well as the seas around the land. However, on to this fourth
world so much rain began to fall that soon even the mountains
were washed away. All the plains were flooded and the whole
land was drowned in a great deluge, turning its people into
fishes.
Then at last the two brother gods, Quetzalcoatl and
Tezcatlipoca, stopped their fighting and together they created
the fifth world, which is our own world. They created the skies

This kneeling statue represents the goddess Chalchiuhtlicue. She was the wife of Tlaloc, the rain god. She was the deity of rivers, lakes and the sea, as well as of the spring water used to irrigate the fields. Mexico is hot and water is often scarce.

Chalchiuhtlicue also played an important role in celebrations for the birth of a child. The midwife welcomed the baby and called on the water goddess to purify the child.

Chalchiuhtlicue wears a jade-green skirt, symbolising fresh water. Aztec people who saw a ritual performer wearing a jade-green skirt would instantly recognise the goddess. Can you think of any modern character in a film or play who can be recognized by what they wear?

and the land, the trees and the flowers as well as the fifth sun, which is the sun of motion and movement. This world, too, may one day be destroyed, not by jaguars or wind, or burning ash or flood, but by the restless mountains around us, and by the thundering of earthquakes beneath our feet.

And so this story comes to an end, little brother, and shows why we must always honor our gods, laying before them gifts and tributes to please them so that they find joy in all our offerings and so that their names will live forever.

The gift of life

We knew that our new sister would be clever with her needle. When we first saw her, her fingers were small, like the tiny plump fish that always slip through the holes of our nets. But because she had been born on the day called One Flower, my mother knew that she would become skilled as an embroiderer. Leaping Frog and I wondered how she could be so sure about this, but she told us that it had always been so and that one day we might even wear cloaks decorated with One Flower's own designs.

Leaping Frog was eager to join in all the celebrations in honor of our sister's birth, and seemed delighted that he would no longer be the youngest child of the family. Secretly, I think that he would have liked my mother's new child to have been a boy so he could have joined the other children running through the streets calling out the name of the future warrior. Still, he was pleased to be given One Flower to hold, before she was passed around between our relatives, neighbors and all the household servants who had joined us for the celebrations.

He certainly enjoyed all the eating and drinking, and listened carefully to the many speeches that were made to welcome our new sister. He seemed fascinated to hear how she was greeted by some of the visitors who called her "Precious Jade" and "Rain Flower" and "Turquoise Maize Flower" and, for once, he even forgot to play his drum! Everybody was anxious to hold the new arrival, and to praise our mother for having become a warrior of childbirth who had taken this new captive, One Flower.

"Did they make speeches like this when I was born?" Leaping Frog asked.

I smiled at him. "You cried all the time so it was hard to listen. But I expect they did."

It wasn't really true about him crying but it is good sometimes to let Leaping Frog know that he is not so important as he thinks he is. Or so perfect as he believes. This time he saw that I was teasing so he just laughed and went on eating more of the honey cakes. Later, he was pleased to watch

The Aztecs enjoyed celebrating the arrival of a new baby. Lots of visitors came and made speeches. This picture from an Aztec book shows what happened at the birth of a boy. Small, curling marks, placed near to mouths, show that people are speaking. In this picture, it seems only the baby was silent! The midwife is carrying the new baby to his ceremonial bath.

Can you spot the miniature examples of things he would use in his future life? A shield and weapons are above the bath. Boys were expected to be warriors. Girls were given a spindle and sweeping brush – you can see these below the bath. Can you think of what kind of presents people would give a new baby today?

as One Flower was ceremonially bathed. He wanted to touch the tiny spindle and sweeping brush placed beside her to show the things she would be using in her life.

I noticed as the feasting went on that Leaping Frog's face had turned pale and that he kept putting his hand on his stomach. As the midwife started on another speech, I saw him move away and go to sit in a corner on his own.

"What's wrong?" I said. "Aren't you going to have any rabbit stew? You've tried everything else. I thought it was your favorite."

Leaping Frog groaned. "I hurt," he said. "I'm going to be sick."

I realized then that he hadn't stopped eating all day, and I was going to tell him how stupid he'd been to eat so many of our neighbor's honey cakes, when he suddenly sprang up and rushed out into the courtyard.

I think he felt better after he'd been sick but I stayed with him because his face was still pale and he didn't want to listen to what the fortune-tellers were saying to my mother about our new sister's future life.

"Don't you want to hear them?" I said.

Leaping Frog shook his head. "How can they see all the things that no one else can see? Anyway, I don't want to know. If the strangers are really coming, they might take One Flower away as a captive."

I stared at him in surprise. I, too, had heard reports of strangers arriving by sea, and I wondered if the trader who had given Leaping Frog his drum had come to confirm such disturbing news. It certainly seemed that even a small boy like Leaping Frog could sense that nothing was as safe and unchanging now as it had been before the rumors had started.

"Fortune-tellers don't know everything," I said. "I know lots of things too. I know a story about how people were first made. Would you like to hear it?"

"Will it make these pains go away?"

"It might," I said, "if you listen properly."

I settled myself comfortably. More neighbors were still arriving, eager to congratulate the family and to welcome One Flower, but as none of them seemed to have noticed us there, I began the story.

The origin of people

Long ago when the two gods Quetzalcoatl and Tezcatlipoca had created the different worlds that came before our present one, they saw that all the people had perished in the great rains and floods that had swept over the land at the time of the last and fourth sun. Some of the people had been turned into fishes and they swam across the great floods of the earth, while all the springs overflowed and the rivers spread. Nowhere could the gods see any men or women. Nor could they see any children.

"There ought to be some people in this new world," said Quetzalcoatl. "There should be humans to live beside its rivers and to travel over its mountains."

"Then we will create them," said Tezcatlipoca. "Together we will make the human beings who are to live in this new land of the fifth sun."

"But how?" said Quetzalcoatl. "How do we do that?"

"You must go down to Mictlan," said Tezcatlipoca, "to the underworld. From there you must bring back some of the bones of the people who lived at the time of the fourth sun. They must be human bones, and must come from that same race that was turned into fish and that lived at the time of the sun of water."

Now both he and his brother knew well who ruled the dangerous place known as Mictlan. It was Mictlantecuhtli himself, the skeletal god of cunning and trickery. However, Quetzalcoatl realized that if new people were to be created, he had to secure those special bones, so he set off at once to make the long journey to the underworld.

There, Mictlantecuhtli was waiting for him with his wife.

Facing them both, Quetzalcoatl said, "I have come to fetch some precious bones that are in your possession. I have come to the underworld because I know that the bones are here."

Mictlantecuhtli did not reply but his wife said, "But why do you need them? What are you going to do with them, Quetzalcoatl?"

"We have created a new world," he replied, "but there are no humans to live there, and no earth should be left empty."

Now the god of death, the cunning Mictlantecuhtli, had

This statue is the god of death, Mictlantecuhtli, who ruled over the underworld. You can see he is wearing a frightening skull mask. Sometimes he is shown as a skeleton wearing a pleated and pointed hat.

Aztecs believed that what happened to you after death depended on how you died, rather than how you lived your life. Courage and self-sacrifice were important to the Aztecs. Brave warriors who died in battle or were sacrificed would go straight to live with the gods. Aztecs thought that women who died while giving birth were brave warriors too. People who died in other ways had to make the long journey to Mictlantecuhtli's kingdom.

been listening carefully and already he had worked out his answer.

"We will give you the bones," he said, "but first you must perform one simple task. You must travel four times around my kingdom of the underworld, and as you go, you must sound a great blast on a conch shell trumpet."

"That will be easy," said Quetzalcoatl. "Give me the trumpet and I will start right away."

Instead of a shell trumpet, the crafty god gave Quetzalcoatl a simple conch with no holes so that it was impossible to make even the smallest of sounds. Quetzalcoatl was not to be beaten. Quickly, he sought out the help of a cluster of worms nearby, asking them to drill some holes in the shell, and when that was done, he called to some bees that were flying by.

"Go into this trumpet," he called, "and make your buzzing into a great roar of sound so that it can be heard throughout the whole realm of the underworld."

Furious at hearing the loud blast on the conch shell trumpet, Mictlantecuhtli had to agree to give up the precious bones. Almost at once, he changed his mind and snatched them back. But he was not quick enough, for in the next instant, Quetzalcoatl had grabbed the bones again and was making his escape.

Even more angry at seeing this, the god of death called to his servants to dig a great pit in the ground, but as Quetzalcoatl ran towards it, a quail, startled by the shouting, suddenly flew out in his path. Quetzalcoatl stumbled and fell, breaking the bones and scattering them around in the bottom of the pit.

Even then, he was determined not to be beaten. Patiently and carefully, Quetzalcoatl collected together every single one of the bones – which were now of many different sizes – and holding them close, he managed at last to carry them out of the underworld. He took them to the miraculous place called Tamoanchan. Here, an old goddess ground the bones into a fine flour which she placed carefully into a special container. Tezcatlipoca and Quetzalcoatl then gave tiny drops of their own blood, letting it fall on the specially-ground flour.

And that was how, from the bones of the fish people mixed with the blood of the gods, we human beings were given life and that's why today, as anyone can see with his own eyes, the people who now live in the Land of the Five Suns are of so many different sizes.

The origin of maize

I could hear the anger in my mother's voice as soon as I came back into the dim light of the house. Everyone else seemed to have disappeared and the place was strangely empty. I knew right away that something was wrong.

I wondered if my mother had heard more rumors about the strangers. The traders who came to my father's house had lately been full of new stories. One of them said that he had seen the strangers with his own eyes. He said he had seen men wearing stone who had come across the sea in giant canoes that had great wings. Even my father seemed to believe him.

I had never seen my father afraid before but he told my mother that he, too, had heard of strange happenings. A fiery serpent had been seen in the sky, and a strange bird had been brought to our great emperor, Moctezuma. Its head was a mirror that showed all the stars of the sky. Even at home there were bad signs. My father's brother had dreamed of a two-headed serpent that was surely a warning of bad trouble, even of death.

After she'd been told these things, my mother watched over One Flower and Leaping Frog far more than she had before, which meant that Leaping Frog always seemed to be in trouble.

He was certainly in trouble now. My mother's eyes were more cold and angry than I had ever seen them before. As I came closer to the hearth, I could hear her threatening Leaping Frog that she would hold him over the fire until its smoke took away his breath. When she saw me, she said that she was far too busy to waste her time on such things, and she went outside into the bright sun and sat down against the wall. I knew then that some of her anger was already fading. It is a strange thing that even when she is angry with any of her children, my mother is never able to remember to punish us as other parents do. Instead, she goes out of the house and sits against the wall, as if she were still a girl living in her father's house.

"What have you done now?" I asked my brother. "Have you been playing your drum instead of gathering wood?"

Aztec parents loved their children but brought them up strictly to prepare them for life. One Aztec book shows some punishments. We don't know if they really did these things or just used them as threats. The book shows children being held over a fire to breathe in stinging chili-pepper smoke or left lying on the cold wet ground. A girl has to sweep all the floors before the sun rises. (Notice the eyes, representing the stars, shown on the drawing).

The grey dots tell you the ages of the children (11, 12, 13 and 14 years). Also shown is the number of tortillas (maize cakes) each is allowed to eat at any meal!

Even small children were expected to help with the work of the household. Do you think that Aztec parents had some good ideas about bringing up children? Would you have liked to live in an Aztec family?

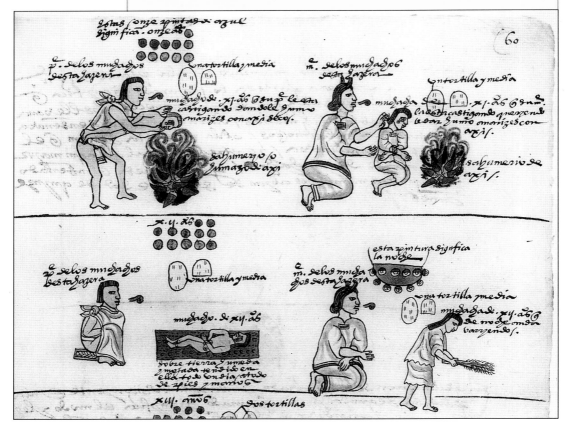

Leaping Frog sighed. "No, I was dancing," he said. "I watched her putting the maize into the cooking pot, blowing on it gently to protect it from the heat of the fire, so I made a dance of my own so that the maize wouldn't be afraid. But I danced too close, and I knocked the pot over and it broke and the maize went straight into the fire. Most of it was lost in the dust and I wanted to run away but I was hungry."

I wanted to laugh but I could see that Leaping Frog would never forget what he had done. Even when he was a man, he would remember when he had wasted food and offended the gods so carelessly. I knew that whenever he watched the planting of the maize seed, or danced at the time of its harvesting, he would never forget the anger in our mother's eyes.

As he sat there, I noticed that an ant was running over one of his toes, and then suddenly I saw a tear from his eyes drop down on to it, washing it aside into the dust. I picked up a piece of straw and held it in front of the ant, and for a moment Leaping Frog stopped his sobbing. The ant paused for a moment and then moved quickly along the length of the straw.

"Do you remember the story about an ant?" I said. "I've told it so many times that I'm sure you must know every word."

Leaping Frog was still frowning. "What if I do?" he said. He had now placed the straw on one of his knees and the ant was beginning the long journey towards his ankle.

"I'm too tired to tell you again," I said. "This time it's your turn."

I thought at first that he was going to refuse but the feel of the ant on his skin was making him smile, so I sat down beside him and, for the very first time, watched Leaping Frog become the storyteller.

Quetzalcoatl and the ant

"I know that's not quite right," said Leaping Frog, "but it's a story about the great god Quetzalcoatl and an ant so that's what I shall call it."

"Storytellers never explain," I said. "They just start and go on until they've finished."

So he did and this is the story he told.

When the gods had finished making all the human beings who were going to live in our land, they knew they were going to have to find something for the people to eat. So they began a great search. They searched and they searched but nowhere could they find any food for the beings they had created.

Then, one day, Quetzalcoatl met a red ant who was carrying a grain of maize. The god saw at once that the maize was just what he was looking for, so he asked the ant where he had found this wonderful grain.

"I won't tell you," said the ant. "Even though you are the great god, Quetzalcoatl, I am not going to answer your question."

Quetzalcoatl was very angry. "How dare you!" he said. "How dare a tiny ant find the courage to speak to a god in this way?"

The ant trembled, for he knew the power of the god and knew how Quetzalcoatl could cause great winds to blow whenever he wished and could destroy all who crossed his path.

Now although this ant was very small, he was also a brave and stubborn ant. "We keep the grain in a secret place," he said, "and I shall never tell you!"

It took Quetzalcoatl a long time to make the ant change his mind. But at last he did, and the ant told him that the grain of maize came from a mountain which was called Mount Tonacatepetl — Mountain of Sustenance. So together they set off to this mountain.

When they reached it, Quetzalcoatl saw at once that only the very smallest of creatures could climb into its center. "There is no way in," he said, "unless I change myself into an ant."

And so he changed himself into a black ant, and he squeezed

and wriggled and squirmed, until at last he managed to follow the red ant through a tiny crack in the rock, deep into the heart of the mountain. Inside, at the very center, was a great chamber, filled with seed and grain up to its high roof. Carefully and slowly, Quetzalcoatl chose a few kernels of the maize and, without dropping a single one, he carried them back to the distant home of the gods.

"This food will give strength to all the people we have created," they said. "We will chew the maize and it will be our gift for all people."

Then the gods said, "What are we going to do with Tonacatepetl, the great mountain, with all its treasure of seeds and grain?"

Quetzalcoatl thought for a moment and then he said, "I shall sling a rope around it and carry it off so that nothing will be lost."

One of the most important Aztec gods is Quetzalcoatl. His name means "quetzal feather serpent." He is often shown partly as a snake and partly as a sacred quetzal bird.

This sculpture of Quetzalcoatl is made of shiny stone which is green like the quetzal bird's feathers. The god has a human head and wears a headdress and splendid jewelry. Can you see his large round ear ornaments and elaborate necklace?

But the mountain was far too heavy to move and it was far too large for anyone to lift. Two of the gods drew lots to decide who should have the seeds, and with the help of the four gods of rain and lightning, they split the mountain wide open so that all the maize kernels and seeds scattered in every direction. Quickly, the four gods, the blue, white, yellow and red Tlalocs, snatched up the seeds of the black, white, yellow and red maize, as well as the seeds for the beans and any of the plants that could be eaten, and they gave them as a gift to all the human beings to use as food.

"And that is how," said Leaping Frog, rising to his feet and looking very important, "the Tlalocs have given us our rain and our crops, and why sometimes even a great god can need the help of an ant." Then he added quickly, "Did I tell it properly?"

As he spoke, I saw that my mother had returned, and that she, too, had been listening.

"Some of the words were not the ones used by most story-tellers," she said. "But I have never heard the story told better or with greater understanding of how the gods gave us maize." And then she paused and smiled. "It also shows just how important it is not to dance too close to the cooking pot, especially when you are feeling hungry."

And Leaping Frog knew that he had been forgiven.

Humming Bird on the Left

I knew that Leaping Frog was still awake. Many times in the night I had heard him leave his mat and go into the courtyard but this time he had not returned. Had he left the house and gone out into the darkness of the city? If he had, then I knew that it was a bad time for me to sleep.

He had pleaded that he should be allowed to go to the Great Temple for the Festival of Huitzilopochtli, our great tribal god who leads us in war and is god of the sun. I realized now that the memory of the day would stay with Leaping Frog for ever. He did not understand yet why we offered all those human lives as a gift to Huitzilopochtli, and why we had eaten those pieces of dough from a large figure made in the god's image.

I had watched his small face all day, as I led him through the crowds towards the moment when the captives started the climb to the top of the high pyramid where their blood was to be shed. I saw his eyes watching the priests, and saw how he stepped back whenever they came near him with their matted hair and their trailing stained robes. I had not been surprised that he came with me willingly when I said that we had to return home.

And now, when it was almost time for the first sight of the morning star, Leaping Frog was still awake.

This powerful-looking knife has a shell and stone mosaic handle shaped like a crouching eagle warrior. It looks like the knives that priests used in sacrifices. They often sacrificed enemy warriors who were captured in battle.

Aztec sacrifices may seem cruel to us, but the Aztecs believed that the sun would not rise and life would not continue if humans didn't thank and please the gods with offerings of blood. They also thought that the sacrificial victims acted as messengers to the gods on their behalf.

I knew that my own eyes would now stay open until I heard the sound of the first temple trumpet of the new day, and I cursed my young brother for all his restless tossing and turning. I could remember, though, the times when I, too, had first been taken to festivals, and of how afterwards my mind had leapt and jumped like a startled rabbit. It had taken a long

Because of the way snakes shed their skins, they are often connected with rebirth and new life. The Aztecs were also impressed by the strength and speed of snakes, which they compared to lightning bolts and fast-flowing water. The earth goddess, Coatlicue, Serpent Skirt, often has snakes around her neck. These snakes probably represent streams of blood.

It is obvious from the accurate carving of this rattlesnake's tongue and fangs that the artist had studied real animals.

time before it became calm again, and before I could forget some of the things I had seen and heard.

So I stopped being angry and I left my mat and went into the courtyard where, in the faint light of the last stars, I saw him standing alone.

"What are you doing?" I said. "I want to sleep. Can't you hear? You've woken the dogs!"

He turned and seemed surprised to see me there.

"I can't sleep," he said. "My mind is full of pictures and they are shouting in my ears."

When I smiled he said angrily, "I want to be a merchant like my father, and if I have to, I will fight like a warrior, but I don't want to do the things the men were doing today." He hesitated. "Will the gods be angry because I say such a thing?"

I put my hand on his shoulder. "I don't know, but this isn't the time for questions, Leaping Frog. It's the time for sleep."

He pulled away from me and moved out of the courtyard.

"Why are they so bright?" he said. "Look – I've never seen them so bright." He was gazing up at the stars as if he had never noticed them before. "Are they really the brothers of Huitzilopochtli? Perhaps they're shining like that because today was his festival. Is that why they're so bright? You must know, Stone Turtle, because you know everything. You said once that the sun god drives them out of the sky every morning with his fiery serpent weapon, and you told me a story about the goddess with the serpent skirt, the one who lived on a mountain. Oh, tell me that story again. If you do I'll go back to my mat and I won't ask you any more questions until it's light."

"Tomorrow I'll tell you," I said. "Not now."

"Then tell me again about the rattlesnake. You said it strikes like an arrow and that you can tell its age by the number of rattles you can count on its tail."

"I only told you that when you found a rattlesnake that day in the courtyard."

"Then tell me about Coatlicue, the one with the serpent skirt."

I could see there would be no sleep for me until the story was told, so we both sat down in the shadows beyond the house so that only Leaping Frog's ears would be the ones to capture the words he was waiting for.

The birth of Huitzilopochtli

It was on the great mountain called Coatepec, that the goddess, Coatlicue, lived and tended the temple that was on its summit. Every day she swept the temple and thought about her four hundred sons who had left her to shine as stars, and about her daughter, who was called Coyolxauhqui. Every day she waited for them to return to her.

Then one day, a feather fell from the sky and fluttered slowly to her feet. It was a very beautiful feather, soft and of many colors. Picking it up, she placed it carefully close to her heart and went on waiting for her sons to return. But they did not come back to her. While she was still waiting, she found she had lost the feather and began to weep. But then her weeping stopped. It stopped because, at that moment, she suddenly realized that she had been chosen to give life to another child, a special child, a child of the gods.

"When my sons come back," she said, "I shall tell them of the strange and wondrous thing that is going to happen," and she sat down there on the mountain and waited with happiness for the return of her children.

But when they came back they were furious. They demanded the name of the father of this child, and threatened to kill their mother. Then, just as they were attacking her,

Coatlicue gave birth to a new son who was the god Huitzilopochtli. This son was not like any other child for he was born fully grown and powerfully strong. Springing forward to defend his mother, he snatched a ray from the sun to use as a weapon. The ray instantly became a fire serpent, and he attacked his brothers, striking his sister, Coyolxauhqui, so fiercely that her body fell in pieces, down, down and down, right to the very foot of the mountain.

Some of his brothers managed to escape and return to the skies, and we can still see them there each day when twilight comes, and can watch each morning when the sun returns to chase them all away.

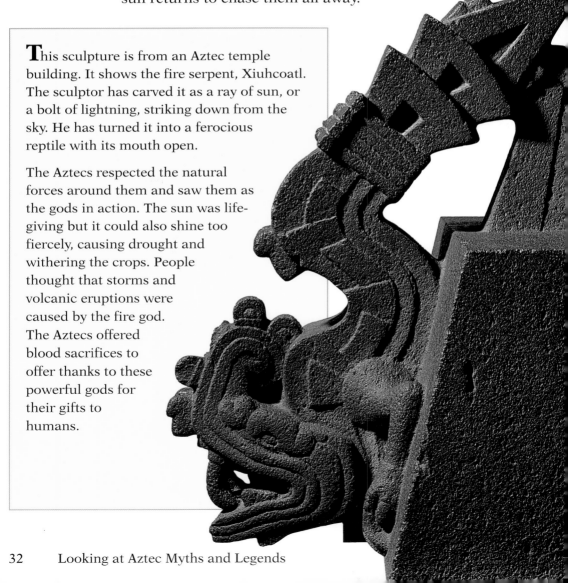

This sculpture is from an Aztec temple building. It shows the fire serpent, Xiuhcoatl. The sculptor has carved it as a ray of sun, or a bolt of lightning, striking down from the sky. He has turned it into a ferocious reptile with its mouth open.

The Aztecs respected the natural forces around them and saw them as the gods in action. The sun was life-giving but it could also shine too fiercely, causing drought and withering the crops. People thought that storms and volcanic eruptions were caused by the fire god. The Aztecs offered blood sacrifices to offer thanks to these powerful gods for their gifts to humans.

I paused, so that Leaping Frog could see for himself that the last of the stars had now disappeared but he had fallen asleep, his head lolling against my arm. I wondered if he was dreaming about all the things he had seen that day. Was he remembering how the women of the city, garlanded in flowers, had danced the serpent dance for the Humming Bird on the Left, whose other name is Huitzilopochtli? So I left him there to listen to the voices of his dreams, hoping that the dog who had stretched out beside him would give him some warmth and stay with him until morning.

After all, there are times when even the telling of stories must come to an end, and everyone knows that when a listener's ears are already closed, there is no longer any need for a storyteller.

A song for a god

Leaping Frog was the first of the children to hear that the traders had returned from their long journey to the coast. He was the one who came running to me to say that our neighbor's house was already crowded with people.

"Our father is there, too," he said, "and many other men. I listened in the doorway but someone saw me there and my father was angry and said I should not have heard the things he was being told."

I looked at Leaping Frog, puzzled. I'd grown used to some of the nonsense he talked but it seemed strange that my father, one of the leaders of the pochteca, the traders of Tenochtitlan, should not want his young son to learn about the life of a merchant. After all, Leaping Frog, once his schooling was over, would be making such journeys himself, bringing back all the wonderful things from distant places that made our great market known throughout the land.

"I don't understand," I said. "What were the traders saying? Why was he so angry?"

Leaping Frog thought for a moment and then said, "I think the news they brought was bad because some of the traders seemed to be afraid and they were asking my father what they should do."

"Why should they be afraid?" I said. "What had they heard?"

Leaping Frog tried to make himself look tall and important. "One of them was the man who gave me my drum. He said he'd seen some of the strangers himself. He said they were carrying pointed sticks that could kill men, sticks that smoked and made a noise like thunder."

"You mean spears?"

"No. These were different. It's true, Stone Turtle. They saw them."

"There are no such sticks," I said. "Next time you should listen with both ears!"

My brother gave me a punch with his small fist. "I heard it all. They said they had met men who had fought with the strangers, and that the strangers were pale, ugly men who had beards, and who rode on hornless deer."

I started to laugh but I could see that even if the rumors were not true, they had made Leaping Frog afraid, and for some reason, they had also made my father angry. The news brought by the traders seemed to be confirming the uneasiness that lately had spread through the markets and streets of Tenochtitlan. Surely nothing could destroy the power and strength of my own people? We Aztecs could command the tribute of gifts and captives from all the other less important cities. I wanted to believe that nothing could threaten the safety of all the people I knew, my friends and family, even the lords of the city, and the great emperor himself, Moctezuma.

It was important now to hide my fear from Leaping Frog.

"Soon our neighbors will be cooking food for a festival for our own god, the god of traders, Yacatecuhtli," I reminded him.

"I know that," said Leaping Frog. "I always go to our neighbor's house when it's a festival for the god of the pochteca. Why should I forget that?"

I tried again. "Last time there were acrobats. They were very clever."

"I know that, too," he said. "I talked to them."

Determined to cheer him up I said, "You told me you were going to practice until you were good enough to join them."

But Leaping Frog still looked unhappy. "I did practice," he said. "I tried juggling a piece of wood with my feet but it was too heavy and it fell on my toes." He was silent for a moment and then he smiled, "If there's music perhaps I could take my drum."

Instantly I promised that there would be music. I could see that he had already forgotten about the travelers and their alarming news so I said quickly, "Shall I tell you the story of how music first began?" I could see from his face that it wasn't a question that needed to be asked.

"I'll go and fetch my drum now," said Leaping Frog, "so don't start till I get back!"

So I didn't.

How music first began

In the far distant times when the gods first created the earth, the winds of the high heavens blew over lands that were silent and where the sound of music was never heard. Though this earth was beautiful with light and color and trees and flowers, its people could hear only silence, and there were no songs to make them happy because no songs had ever been sung.

That was how it was when the god Tezcatlipoca, the Smoking Mirror, came down to earth one day and found a great sadness wherever he looked. Nowhere could he find any musicians or songs or people dancing, however far he traveled. He searched in the mountains and in the valleys, but everywhere the men's voices were silent and his ears heard only the sound of the wind and the great roar of the oceans.

Returning again to his brother, Quetzalcoatl, he told him how the earth was weary of its own silence, and he ordered Quetzalcoatl to make a journey to the House of the Sun, which is the place where all life begins.

"We must give them music," he said. "They are tired of being sad. That is why you must go to our father, the sun, who is surrounded by the makers of music, and take a few of them back to Earth."

"But I shall need a bridge to reach the House of the Sun," said Quetzalcoatl. "There is no bridge that can take me to the roof of the world."

Tezcatlipoca assured him that three of his own servants would help to make a bridge. "Their names are Cane and Conch, Water Woman, and Water Monster, and they will come to meet you on the very edge of the seashore."

Sure enough, as Quetzalcoatl reached the edge of the sea, the three servants came forward to help him. Entwining their three bodies, they made a bridge for him to pass over to continue his journey to the sun.

Playing music, singing and dancing were important to the Aztecs. But even before the Aztec empire existed, other peoples in ancient Mexico made music using percussion and wind instruments. This pottery figure of a drummer comes from West Mexico. It was made hundreds of years before the Aztecs built Tenochtitlan.

Aztec children were taught ritual and religious songs and dances in schools called Houses of Song. They learned how to play different kinds of instruments, including drums, shell trumpets, flutes, bells and whistles.

As he went further into the high heavens, the sun saw him approaching and called all his musicians together to give them a warning.

"Stop all your music," he told them. "Make no sound and when Quetzalcoatl calls, do not answer him."

The musicians, who had been very happy living on the heavenly roof of the world among all the melodies and songs, had no wish to leave such a place of light and happiness so they did exactly what they were told. As Quetzalcoatl came nearer, the sun warned them again.

"Silence all your flutes," he said, "and ignore his words when he calls. If you follow him down the stairways of light back to the earth you will have to stay down there for ever."

Then Quetzalcoatl spoke and the musicians trembled as they heard his powerful voice. "Come with me, musicians. Can't you hear me, all you singers? The supreme Lord of the World is calling you. Why won't you answer?"

He waited, and still they gave him no answer.

He called to them again and then again, until he grew angry and began to toss aside the clouds, throwing daggers of lightning and making the heavens dark with a terrible thunder.

Still nobody answered him, and then when at last the skies were quiet again, one of the musicians relented. Raising his voice, he spoke to the waiting god. "We will come with you," he said. "We'll leave the House of the Sun and take our songs down to the earth if that is what must be done."

Contented and happy, Quetzalcoatl collected together a few of the musicians, and bearing them very gently so that he didn't hurt any of the melodies, he started on the long journey back to earth where a great welcome was waiting for them. Even the trees lifted their branches, and the wind fluttered the feathers of the quetzal birds and opened the petals of the flowers as every being in the land began to sing.

That is how music was born, and why, since that day, men have always sung and played their flutes, listening with happiness to the melodies that were given to them by the gods, the melodies that drove away the long silence for ever.

The coming of light

L eaping Frog was in trouble again.

I could hear that my mother was angry with him as soon as I woke.

"You are not old enough to go to school," I heard her say. "Why do you worry me so? You will go to school when it is time for you to go. And not before."

"But all my brothers go and they learn everything that I want to learn. That is why Stone Turtle knows so many stories. And he knows about history and the stars and ..."

My mother interrupted him. "Because he was born before you were and never pestered me with questions like this. Now go and fetch me more wood and keep your tongue still before you wake One Flower with all your complaining."

Later, when I set off for school, I could see Leaping Frog still sitting on his favorite stone in the yard where the turkeys live. He always goes there when he's feeling unhappy, though I know he's often afraid when the birds make a noise and move too close. But if he sits in the yard, he can pretend that he can't hear our mother calling him above the noise of the turkeys.

I waved to him but he turned his head away and stared down at the dust, pretending he hadn't seen me. Then I saw my mother taking him a piece of fruit and knew that they had finished their quarreling and that she would forget to be angry with him until the next time he worried her with questions. I had enough questions of my own and was anxious to find out what was to happen in the school that day. In the past weeks things had felt different. Some of the boys I had grown up with had already gone to join their fathers as warriors, and several of our teachers had disappeared. Somehow school no longer seemed important. All of us knew that if our great city needed to be defended, each one of us would have to become a warrior but, despite all the rumors already reaching Tenochtitlan, it still felt too soon to speak of such things.

It was not until I returned home again that I heard that Leaping Frog had disappeared and that no one in the household had seen him all day. It was a bad time for a boy on his own to wander through the city streets, so I promised my mother that I would set off at once to look for him. I tried the markets first but found all the stall-holders already packing up their goods before the light faded. I remembered that Leaping Frog knew some of the featherworkers in the market but none of them had seen him that day.

"Why is your brother such a wanderer?" one of the men said. "Every day there is someone looking for Leaping Frog but he is always found so why do you worry about him now? No child will stay alone to face the spirits in such darkness."

I hadn't noticed that it was so late but I was sure that the man was wrong about my brother. He didn't know Leaping Frog as well as I did. Even though we all feared the blackness of the

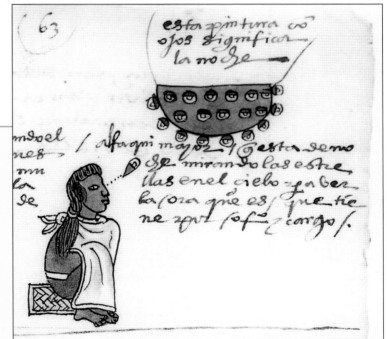

This picture from an Aztec book shows a scholar studying the night sky and the stars. Most boys from wealthy families like Stone Turtle went to schools run by priests. They studied astronomy, as well as music, mathematics, religion and history. One book calls the schools "houses of tears" because the boys had to work so hard!

In Aztec times, just like now, parents wanted their children to have the best possible education for a successful life. What children did depended on their family's wealth and position as well. Stone Turtle expected to become a merchant like his father.

city at night, I felt sure that Leaping Frog must have some plan or other that would prevent him from running home before carrying it out. But what sort of plan could it be this time? I remembered then the morning's argument with my mother. If he couldn't become a pupil at my own school, perhaps he thought he could try another. Suddenly I thought of the Temple School near the center of the city. Two of our sisters had been sent there to train as temple helpers. Leaping Frog might have thought they would let him stay there too. If so, there was no time to be lost.

I began to hurry, glancing up at the distant pyramid of the Great Temple, topped with the temples of the two gods, Tlaloc and Huitzilopochtli. Then I heard the sound of voices and thought I could make out the shape of two men, their faces turned away from me. There was someone else with them and I saw that it was Leaping Frog trying to escape from the grasp of two priests. I knew he hadn't seen me but before I could call out, he managed to free himself. I could hear his gasps as he ran. I thought at first that one of the men was going to follow, but he turned away and disappeared into the sacred precinct of the Great Temple.

Leaping Frog was already far ahead of me, running through the darkness in wild panic, but at last I caught up with him and grabbed at his shoulder. He gave a scream and then stumbled so that I, too, tripped and fell.

"It's only me," I said. "It's all right. It's only me."

"I thought you were a spirit. I thought you were a bad spirit."

For a moment, I wanted to make him tell me why he had run away and what it was that made him so desperate to start his school learning, but I didn't like the darkness myself, certainly not the darkness in this part of the city where so many captives had been sacrificed and so much blood spilt. Leaping Frog was right. The spirits were all around us and we were far from our own hearth.

"Come on. Get on my back," I said. "We'll pretend you're a basket of fish."

As I spoke, the ground under our feet was suddenly patterned with silver, and when we looked up, we saw the moon, the lovely Lady Golden Bells, move out from behind some clouds. Leaping Frog seemed to forget his fear and I saw him smiling. "Now I can be a basket of silver fish," he said, "and you can tell me that story again about the sun and the moon."

"I don't remember it." Looking round, I saw that Tenochtitlan had become my own city again, the shape of its houses and trees now clearly visible in the new light, no longer a place of darkness, but the familiar home of all my friends and my family.

"Yes, you do," said Leaping Frog. "You do remember it."

And, of course, I did.

The creation of the sun and moon

Now in the very beginning when there was darkness, all the gods gathered together to decide who was going to be the one who would give the world its sun and all its light. A great fire was lit, and one of the most splendid gods said that he would sacrifice himself by leaping on to the fire to become the sun. In preparation, this god, whose name was Tecuciztecatl, began to lay out all his fine garments to wear for the sacrifice, but then another god stepped forward. His name was Nanahuatzin and he was very poor and had boils all over his face. Unlike Tecuciztecatl, he had no rich incense or quetzal feathers or gold to give as offerings, but only bundles of reeds and pieces of his own skin.

However, the two gods prepared themselves for the ceremony and spent four nights in penance so that they should be worthy of the honor of becoming the sun. At last, at midnight on the fifth night, all the gods gathered at the fire to watch Tecuciztecatl throw himself on to its flames. But the heat was so unbearable that the god was afraid and drew back. The gods who were watching waited for him to try again, but the second time, he could not find the courage, and even on the third and fourth attempts, he could not bring himself to let the fire consume him.

"Take courage," the other gods called. "Throw yourself into the flames."

This mask may have been worn by a man impersonating an Aztec god during a sacred ceremony. No one is sure which god this mask represented, but there are some clues!

Can you see several boil-like bumps on the face of the mask? That means he could be the god Nanauatzin, who is in this story.

Can you also see the shape of a butterfly on its cheeks where a darker coloured stone has been used? The butterfly is the emblem of the Mexican fire god, whose name means Turquoise Lord. Butterflies are also symbols of the souls of brave warriors.

We may never know for sure how this mask was used or whom it represented.

Still Tecuciztecatl held back and turned away from the pile of glowing coals. But the poor little god Nanahuatzin came forward bravely, and without pausing, threw himself on to the fire. Shamed by this sacrifice, Tecuciztecatl quickly followed him into the flames, and as the gods burned, an eagle and a jaguar leapt on to the fire too.

The other gods watched and waited, not knowing which god was going to give them the first dawn. And they continued to wait, looking in every direction until at last those who had been looking to the east saw light beginning to spread, growing brighter and brighter until the newly created sun itself burst into the sky. It was Nanahuatzin! The sun almost blinded them with its light, and its brilliant rays spread across the earth.

Then, as they watched, they saw Tecuciztecatl rise from the fire, in the form of a second sun, just as brilliant as the first. The gods decided that the world might be far too bright with these two great suns, so one of them threw a rabbit across the face of the second one, which made it dimmer than the sun for ever. Since then, men have been able to see the imprint of a rabbit on their moon to remind them that it had once been a sun.

This small carving of an eagle warrior is made of precious green jade. Two important groups in the Aztec army were the Eagles and Jaguars, named after the two brave animals who sacrificed themselves with the gods.

Both nobles and commoners could reach high rank by bravery in battle, especially by capturing enemy warriors. High-ranking warriors wore special headgear, jewelry and cloaks. Jaguar warriors wore jaguar skins.

Warriors were trained in the special "Eagle House" schools. They learned how to use javelins, clubs and shields. They learned, too, about past battles and the history and traditions of their order.

Can you see the eagle headdress on the jade figure?

The gods then saw that the sun and moon were still not moving so, to set them both in motion, they sacrificed themselves on the fire. Instantly the sun began to move across the sky, and when its first crossing had been completed, the moon chose its own path, and both of them went on their own way. So it is that, just as the gods sacrificed themselves, humans must offer their hearts and their blood to ensure that the fifth sun can continue to follow its path.

Even today, the jaguar and eagle, who followed the gods into the flames, still carry the signs of their courage in the sooty markings of their coats and their smut-stained feathers. Their courage is honored by the dress of our brave jaguar and eagle knights when they fight in battle or are taken as captives, reminding us again of how we were given our sun and moon, and how the first dawn was created.

Arrival of the strangers

The day we had been dreading had at last arrived! The strangers were here, were actually here in our own city, walking in the streets of Tenochtitlan.

Yet, instead of the fighting and slaughter we had expected, we had seen our emperor, the Great Speaker himself, Moctezuma, welcome them with fine speeches. Wearing his quetzal bird plumes, his turquoise headdress, and his jade and gold jewels, he had been borne forward in splendor to meet the lord of the strangers. There had even been an exchange of gifts between them that I had seen with my own eyes.

Leaping Frog had been angry that he had not been allowed to join the crowds, too, so when I came home again, he was the first person I wanted to tell about the amazing happenings of the day. But I found the whole house in an uproar, with the family and servants frantically scurrying in all directions. Many traders had come to talk with my father and I knew they would be arguing all night about what they had seen.

To my surprise, I found my mother slowly and graciously handing frothing drinks of chocolate to the men as if it were just a day like any other day. Silenced by her calmness, I watched her starting to pound yet another bowl of the cacao beans. Leaping Frog was watching her, too, and later she let him sip the last of the froth as she poured it from one bowl to the other before adding the maize gruel and flavoring of vanilla. As he drank, Leaping Frog's cheeks glistened with froth and there was a beard of small bubbles across his chin.

"When you drink chocolate," she said, "you should open your mouth wide like a bird in the nest."

"I know that," said Leaping Frog. "But I forgot because I was thinking about today when all my older brothers went with my father to see the strangers arrive and I had to stay here by the hearth with One Flower."

My mother frowned. "All day you have been complaining! What do you know about men who come from other places? How do any of us know what is in the heart of a stranger?" Suddenly angry, she turned on Leaping Frog.

"Leave me," she said. "Go! I am tired of the sound of your voice."

Startled by such fury, Leaping Frog fled, and I, too, left her, anxious not to anger her any more. I knew she still had doubts about the wisdom of welcoming those strangers, and secretly I felt the same. So I took my time in finding Leaping Frog, but in the end I discovered him sitting at the foot of his favorite tree in the orchard.

"She'll be making more chocolate later," I said, "but remember next time to open your mouth wide."

The thought of another drink seemed to cheer him and I was pleased when he pulled me down to sit beside him.

"I've forgotten the story," he said, "but you told me once that one of the gods gave us chocolate. But I don't remember which one."

I knew that he remembered quite clearly and probably could have recited every word. I was pleased, though, that he had cheered up, so I leaned back against the tree and began the story.

The origin of chocolate

Now in the time when Quetzalcoatl lived with all his brothers in the home of the gods, he had noticed that there was a certain tree that was not like any of the other trees. It stood alone and from its branches hung strange long pods which held many seeds. Quetzalcoatl watched the tree grow and he watched as it flourished and blossomed, while all the time the butterflies and birds flew among its leaves and flowers. He watched it until one day he knew that he must taste its seeds, for in those seeds lay all the secrets of wisdom and learning.

So, one day, without telling his brother gods, he stole the tree and took it to the sacred place called Tula where he planted it deep into the soil. But as he watched, the tree's leaves curled and withered, and all its flowers turned brown and died, and he knew that unless he asked for help, the seeds of wisdom would be lost for ever.

Swallowing his pride, Quetzalcoatl went first to the great god of rain, whose name was Tlaloc.

"My tree will die," he said, "unless you feed it with your rain and give it life. Please, Tlaloc, please save my tree."

So Tlaloc, who lived high above the forest, called together his servants and created a great thunderstorm that rumbled and crashed around the mountaintops and threw driving rain over the empty branches of Quetzalcoatl's tree. And the tree spread its roots deep and drank the new rain so that soon fresh leaves began to sprout. But still it bore no flowers and still there was no sign of the pods that would bear the seeds of wisdom.

"I must go to ask the help of Xochiquetzal, the goddess of flowers," thought Quetzalcoatl, and he traveled to the home of the goddess.

"Please help me, Precious Feather Flower," said Quetzalcoatl. "Please scatter some flowers over my tree."

And the goddess gathered together all the petals that were needed, and threw them among the leaves of the tree until it looked exactly as Quetzalcoatl had seen it in the home of the gods. Then, as soon as the new pods had ripened, he collected its seeds and showed the women of that place the way they could be dried in the sun, and ground to make the drink of chocolate.

I paused then in the story, surprised by the stillness of Leaping Frog, only to find that he was fast asleep. The orchard was already dark, but I could still hear my father's voice and knew that there would be little sleep in our home that night. I looked across at the city and thought again of the strangers. What was there to fear after all? Surely Tenochtitlan was the great center of our empire, a city more powerful than any other? The arrival of a few strangers could not make any difference.

   Pulling my brother closer into the warmth of my cloak, I shut my eyes and waited for the first sign of the new dawn.

This red stone statue represents the god Xochipilli. His name means Flower Prince. Xochipilli is the male partner of Xochiquetzal, the goddess of flowers. There were often two Aztec gods, one male and one female, who were responsible for similar things. Xochipilli was also the patron of pleasure and feasting, dancing, games and painting.

We have met many of the Aztec gods in these stories. Can you remember some of them and what they did? Good luck with the spelling!

Further reading

Books about the Aztecs:
E. Baquedano, *Eyewitness Guide: Aztec*, Dorling Kindersley 1993
P. Bateman, *Aztecs Activity Book*, British Museum Press 1994
P. Hicks, *Look into the Past: The Aztecs*, Wayland 1993

Other books about ancient Mexican peoples:
P. Chrisp, *The Maya: Look into the Past*, Wayland 1994
D. Gifford, *Warriors, Gods and Spirits from Central and South American Mythology*, Peter Lane (Eurobook) 1983
S.A. Savage, *Ancient Maya Temples to Make*, Stemmer House Publishers, Inc. 1987
L. Watson (editor), *A Mayan Town Through History*, Wayland 1994

The pictures

BM = By courtesy of the Trustees of the British Museum

pp 4-5	BM Ethno. 1894-634
p.9	Codex Mendoza, MS Arch. Seld. A.1 fol. 2r. Bodleian Library, Oxford.
p.11	BM Ethno. 1949 Am 22.218
p.14	BM Ethno. St. 401
p.16	BM Ethno. 1825.12-10.6
p.18	Codex Mendoza, MS Arch. Seld. A.1 fol. 57r. Bodleian Library, Oxford
p.21	BM Ethno. 1849.6-29.2
p.24	Codex Mendoza, MS Arch. Seld. A.1 fol. 60r. Bodleian Library, Oxford.
p.27	BM Ethno. 1825.12-10.11
p.29	BM Ethno. St. 399
p.32	BM Ethno.1825.12-10.1
p.36	BM Ethno. Hn.26
p. 39	Codex Mendoza, MS Arch. Seld. A.1 fol. 63r Bodleian Library, Oxford.
pp 42	BM Ethno. St. 400
p.43	BM Ethno. 1856.4-22.93
p.47	BM Ethno. 1825.12-10.5